THIS CANDLEWICK BOOK BELONGS TO:

Cheryl Jones

Kenneth Lilly's
ANIMALS

For my family K.L.

Text copyright © 1988 by Joyce Pope
Illustrations copyright © 1988 by Kenneth Lilly

Second U.S. edition 1995

Library of Congress Cataloging-in-Publication Data

Lilly, Kenneth. [Animals]
Kenneth Lilly's animals / text by Joyce Pope.
Originally published: London : Walker Books, 1988. Includes index.
Summary: Text and illustrations introduce a variety of animals from
different topographical areas around the world.
ISBN 1-56402-513-6
1. Animals —Juvenile literature.   [1. Animals.]   I. Pope, Joyce.
II. Title.   III. Title: Animals.
QL49.L668   1995
599— dc20   94-5309

2 4 6 8 10 9 7 5 3 1

Printed in Hong Kong

The pictures in this book were done in watercolor.

Candlewick Press
2067 Massachusetts Avenue
Cambridge, Massachusetts 02140

Kenneth Lilly's
ANIMALS

Wildlife Around the World

Text by Joyce Pope

CANDLEWICK PRESS
CAMBRIDGE, MASSACHUSETTS

Contents

HOT FORESTS

More different species of animals live in the world's hot forests than in any other kind of habitat. Yet if you were to visit one of the great forests that grow near the equator, you would probably see very few animals. There are many different kinds of trees, their huge trunks rising like the pillars of a cathedral until, perhaps 100 feet above, they spread out into a green canopy of branches and leaves. This casts a deep shade, so few plants grow on the ground. Fallen fruits, flowers, and leaves provide food for some ground-dwelling animals that are usually small and difficult to see. The majority of hot forest animals, however, live up in the web of branches. Most of them are climbers and fliers: Monkeys, sloths, squirrels, and bats share their sunlit world with gorgeously colored birds, such as parrots, hummingbirds, toucans, and birds of paradise, and brilliantly colored insects, including beetles and butterflies. There is always plenty of food for them in the treetops, because near the equator there is rain every day and the trees grow throughout the year. Although individual trees lose their leaves from time to time, in any one month there will be some trees in flower and others in fruit.

11

Gorilla
Gorilla gorilla

A baby gorilla, like a human baby, is almost completely helpless when it is born. Its mother carries it all the time, protecting it and feeding it on her milk. When it is three months old, the baby starts to crawl, and at six months begins to climb and play with other youngsters in the family group. Female gorillas do not have another baby for several years, so there are not many playmates of equal age. But all gorillas, even the biggest males—called silverbacks—are very gentle with the young ones.

Gorillas wake up at about six o'clock in the morning. They are choosy feeders and look, in a leisurely way, for the leaves and stems of their favorite plants. They rarely take anything else, not even insects or honey. At about ten o'clock they rest, snoozing into early afternoon, when they wake to feed again. At dusk they make nests of broken and roughly woven branches either on the ground or in low trees. Although they climb well, gorillas spend most of the time on the ground.

Despite their peaceful way of life, gorillas have been attacked by humans and are among the world's endangered animals. In some areas they are now protected, but their survival depends also upon the preservation of their forest home.

Okapi
Okapia johnstoni

The okapi is a mystery animal. It was not seen alive by Europeans until 1900, which makes it one of the last big animals to be discovered. The reason for this is that okapis live in dense, damp forests, which are difficult and dangerous to explore; okapis are well camouflaged in this leafy habitat. They usually live alone or in small groups, and have such a marvelous sense of hearing that they bolt at any unusual sound. Okapis are related to giraffes, but are much smaller. Like giraffes, the males have small hair-covered horns, and all okapis have very long tongues—so long that they can lick and clean their own eyes. Babies are born between April and October, the rainiest part of the year. They weigh about 35 lbs. and are soon eating leaves and fruit like their parents.

13

Tiger
Panthera tigris

A baby tiger is unlikely to know its father, as it is cared for and brought up entirely by its mother. She chooses the safe place in which her litter of up to six cubs is born, and feeds them on milk for about the first six months of their lives. After this, they begin to follow her on hunting expeditions, becoming skilled in using their senses of hearing and sight to track the deer and other large animals that are their prey. By the time they are one year old, the youngsters can make kills themselves. But they still have much to learn, so the family stays together for at least another year. Like all cats, tiger cubs play with each other, but as they grow up, they wander away to live on their own. They do not seem to want company, and each tiger occupies a huge territory, avoiding its neighbors if possible, even though it knows who they are.

Tigers usually live among trees, where they are well camouflaged. Unlike most other cats, they like water and often lie in it during hot weather. At one time, tigers were found in many parts of Asia, even in the cold forests of Siberia, but hunting and forest-clearing have seriously reduced their numbers. In 1920 the tiger population was estimated at 100,000 animals; it is now less than 3,000.

Gibbon
Hylobates agilis

Gibbons are animals of the treetops. On long slender arms and legs, they swing and leap through the forest, sometimes covering more than 25 feet in a single bound. Their long, narrow hands act like hooks, grabbing branches to support them as they pass. Gibbons know their upper-storey living places very well, as each family lives in and defends quite a small area of forest.

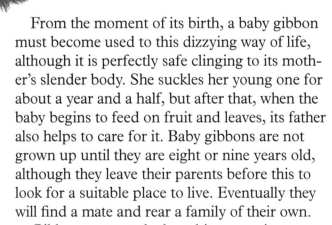

From the moment of its birth, a baby gibbon must become used to this dizzying way of life, although it is perfectly safe clinging to its mother's slender body. She suckles her young one for about a year and a half, but after that, when the baby begins to feed on fruit and leaves, its father also helps to care for it. Baby gibbons are not grown up until they are eight or nine years old, although they leave their parents before this to look for a suitable place to live. Eventually they will find a mate and rear a family of their own.

Gibbons are not the least bit aggressive. Treetop neighbors never fight. Instead, they yodel and call to warn others off, making sounds that travel long distances through the trees.

Orangutan
Pongo pygmaeus

The orangutan, unlike the gibbon, lives in the lower branches and moves slowly through the forest. Apart from mothers with babies, orangutans generally live alone, although youngsters, when they first set out on their own, occasionally join up with others of the same age for a short time. A baby is not weaned until it is three, and in its first year is never separated from its mother.

Orangutans lead leisurely lives. They sleep at night in large nests made of roughly woven branches and often make smaller nests for their midday rest. In the morning and afternoon they feed, mainly on fruit. They are particularly fond of wild figs, but also eat leaves, buds, and insects. They seem not to like heavy rain, and will drape large leaves around their shoulders or hold leafy branches over their heads for protection.

Orangutans live a very long time—the record is fifty-nine years—yet they are becoming rarer in the wild as their forest homes are destroyed.

Slender loris
Loris tardigradus

Slender lorises are rarely seen in the wild, for they are solitary animals of the night. After dark they emerge from their hiding places and move stealthily through the forest canopy. The loris progresses slowly and cautiously, shifting one limb at a time, while holding on tight with the other three. Its large eyes and ears help it to locate insects or other small animals, and, when it is close enough, it grabs with both hands together to catch the prey. A loris's teeth are suited not only for crunching the hard shells of insects or birds' eggs, but also for cleaning its soft, woolly fur. The lower front teeth stick forward, making a fine comb. And one toe on each hind foot has a special claw that the loris also uses for grooming, so it is well equipped to keep itself neat and tidy.

Slender lorises do not make nests, but each male occupies an area of forest that overlaps the range of several females. Males recognize females by their scent trails and seek them out during the mating season. Usually one baby is born at a time. The thickly furred newborn loris clings to its mother while she searches for food at night, but as it grows she forages alone, leaving the baby holding tightly to a branch.

Spotted cuscus
Phalanger maculatus

At first sight a cuscus looks like a furry, woolly monkey, but this slow-moving inhabitant of forest and thick scrub is a marsupial, or pouched animal, more closely related to the kangaroos than to the apes. During the day, cuscuses lie curled up in a safe place. At night they travel through the trees, looking for the fruit, insects, and birds' eggs that are their main food. They have catlike eyes with pupils that shrink to a narrow slit in the light but open wide to help them see in the dark. Although they are solitary creatures, cuscuses produce a penetrating, musky smell so that, though they rarely meet, males and females can keep track of each other.

One or sometimes two young are born a few weeks after the adults mate. At birth, a baby cuscus is barely larger than a coffee bean, but it scrambles through its mother's fur to her pouch, where it finds the milk that enables it to grow in warmth and safety for the next six months. Only males develop a spotted coat.

Like many other tree-climbers, a cuscus can spread its toes wide to grasp the branches. In addition, the undersides of its feet are like nonslip soles of bare, ridged skin and its tail is prehensile, which means it can grip. The tail also helps the cuscus to balance. The toes of the hind feet have yet another function: Two of them have extra-long claws so that cuscuses have a comb with which to groom themselves.

Scarlet macaw
Ara macao

Scarlet macaws feed on fruits and seeds in the treetops of tropical forests. As they sway on the sunlit branches, these magnificent birds look like huge, brightly colored flowers. Macaws enjoy each other's company, and parties of up to twenty birds may be seen together. Males and females are so alike in appearance that it is difficult to tell them apart, although it is easy to spot birds that have formed pairs, since they always keep very close to each other. When they leave the food trees to go to their roosts, which are often some way off, the paired birds fly so close together that their wing tips almost touch.

The nests of scarlet macaws have rarely been found but are, apparently, generally high above the ground in hollow trees. It is likely that a pair may use the same breeding site for several years. Like all baby parrots, macaw nestlings are helpless and need to be fed by their parents for some time. It seems that they get infrequent— though probably rather large—meals. Once they are fledged, young macaws still remain with their parents and have even been seen near the nest in which the next year's chicks are being reared.

Scarlet macaws are now far rarer than they used to be. Not only is their forest home being destroyed but—as the birds will not readily breed in captivity—macaws are too frequently and indiscriminately captured for the pet trade.

Chimpanzee
Pan troglodytes

A chimpanzee has all its mother's attention for at least the first four years of its life, as she will not have another baby during that time. At first, the infant clings to its mother's chest; later it rides on her back. When it has become adventurous enough to leave her side, there are other chimps to look after it: among them, most likely, an older brother or sister, as chimps often remain with their mother until they are ten.

Chimpanzees usually move around in small parties, although these may belong to a group of up to eighty animals that occupies a large area of forest. Patrolling males warn off neighboring groups by leaping around, screaming, or breaking branches in a dramatic display of ferocity. But there is little serious fighting within a group, and even adult males feed together and groom each other.

By day, chimpanzees search the ground for fruit, leaves, eggs, honey, and insects, including termites, which they "fish" from mounds with blades of grass or twigs. Occasionally they kill and eat monkeys and small antelopes. At night, chimps retreat to the safety of the trees, each one weaving a springy mattress of leaves and branches about 30 feet above the ground.

Indian elephant
Elephas maximus

The Indian elephant is slightly smaller than its African cousin. Even so, it is the second largest land animal by a long way. A newborn Indian elephant weighs about 225 lbs. and has a coat of coarse, fuzzy hair. As it grows up, this becomes less noticeable, and an adult elephant not only seems to be hairless, but often looks bright red or brown. This is because elephants like to give themselves dust baths, or to wallow in brightly colored mud.

An elephant breathes through its trunk, which is really a nose, and uses it to drink by sniffing up water and then squirting it into its mouth. The tip of the trunk is so sensitive that it can pick a single berry, and so strong that it can break branches. Indian bull elephants can also have big tusks, but females rarely do.

Adult elephants eat vast quantities of leaves and grasses, feeding morning, evening, and night. Although males are often found alone, females always live in herds. A baby remains in the group until it is at least ten years old. It could live to be eighty, but few do so today, as the Indian elephants' habitat is threatened.

COOL FORESTS

Trees must have lots of water if they are to grow well. Apart from in the tropics, heavy rain falls over much of Europe and in a band stretching across Asia and a good deal of North America. At one time vast forests grew in this wet zone around the world. There are also forests in the cool southern parts of South America, in New Zealand, and in Australia. Now, especially in Europe, much of the forest has been felled and the land used for farming. The remaining trees form woodlands very different from those of the tropics. There are fewer kinds of trees—often one type will dominate a large area. Nor do the trees grow throughout the year. Deciduous trees lose their leaves in autumn. Evergreens, with their small, hard leaves, are protected against frost and snow, but they too are dormant in the cold winter months.

Fewer kinds of animals live in these cool woodlands, but as in the hot forests, many of them are climbers and fliers. Martens hunt squirrels among the branches. Birds such as the acrobatic titmouse eat insects and spiders hiding among the leaves; woodpeckers dig out grubs from beneath the bark, while nutcrackers, crossbills, finches, and jays feed on the seeds. There are more big ground-dwelling animals than in the tropical forests. Deer and bears are the largest; there are also many members of the weasel family, including badgers and skunks. Besides these, mice, voles, and shrews scurry around to feed or hunt—small animals that are active through much of the day and night.

Roe deer
Capreolus capreolus

Camouflaged by the dappled light falling on its spotted coat, the roe deer kid lies so still that most of its enemies pass it by. In fact, there may be two babies resting on the woodland floor, as roe deer often produce twins. The babies are not lost, however, and their mother is almost certainly nearby. She leaves her kids hidden like this because, although they can stand and even walk within minutes of being born, they cannot run well if there is any threat of danger. The doe will return to feed them in the evening and again in the early morning, which are the times that deer are most active. In the autumn, the kids exchange their spotted baby coats for the grayish-brown winter coloring of the adults. By this time they are almost weaned, and feed on brambles and other leaves, as well as on acorns and fruit. They even raid farmers' fields.

In a hard winter, roe deer may congregate in loose herds. Only males grow antlers. These look like horns, but unlike horns, antlers are shed and regrown each year. They are mainly used to spread scent from facial glands and as weapons of defense.

Moose

Alces alces

Like roe deer, moose mothers often produce twins, although the moose calf does not have a spotted coat. Newborn babies spend at least the first two weeks of life hidden in the undergrowth. After that, they are able to follow their mother and browse on twigs of alder and willow, which grow in the moist places where moose prefer to spend the summer months. They may even venture into ponds or lakes, ducking their heads underwater to find the stems and roots of water lilies, which are a favorite food.

In winter, groups of moose migrate to places where the snowfall is light enough for them to paw through it to find food. They also eat the twigs and bark of conifers. When spring comes, the groups break up again, as moose are more solitary than most large deer. At this time, the yearlings are driven off by their mothers, who need to devote all their attention to the new babies. The young moose remain in the area and may rejoin their mother once her calves are a few weeks old. But after the next winter they find a different place to live and, in the following year, may have calves of their own.

Red fox
Vulpes vulpes

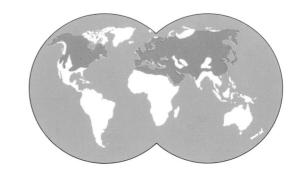

The nursery for red fox cubs is a secluded den made by their mother. When they are first born, the cubs are blind and helpless and the vixen stays with them all the time, feeding them milk and keeping them warm.

After about a month the cubs venture into the outside world. At first they are uncertain on their legs, but soon they become stronger and more agile. At this age the cubs spend most of their time playing. Their games are always mock battles, but in these contests they learn the skills that they must have when they are grown up, for they discover how to attack and how to defend themselves. The cubs are protected and fed by both parents. Sometimes one of them will bring an injured animal—a moorhen or a mole, perhaps—to the den, so that the cubs can practice making a real kill. The family stays together until the end of the summer, but in early autumn the cubs wander away to find a home of their own.

At first they may not be good hunters, but this does not matter much, as foxes will eat almost anything. They may live on blackberries or windfall apples, insects, and worms. But they prefer meat and when possible will feed on mice and rats. Some foxes learn to raid henhouses, but most do not, as they are very wary, although they are less afraid of humans than most wild animals are. Perhaps this is one of the reasons for their success: Foxes manage to survive in many kinds of living places, even in some big towns, although they are more at home in wooded countryside.

Raccoon
Procyon lotor

Unlike fox cubs, which start life underground, raccoons are born in a hollow tree in a den at least 10 feet above ground. Perhaps because of the danger of falling, they do not leave the den until they are about two months old, when their mother takes them to another lair, this time on the ground. Soon after this, they begin to follow her for short distances, often to new homes, as raccoons like to keep on the move. They rarely travel far, but have a number of safe places in their territory, each of which will be used for a few days at a time. The main exception to this is during a cold spell, when they prefer to live on their fat rather than go out and face freezing winter weather.

Raccoons are good swimmers as well as good climbers and are often found near water. They eat crabs, crayfish, frogs, and fish, and also fruits and seeds. Some raccoons have found that not all humans are enemies: The animals sleep by day in lofts and barns, and at night scavenge the rich pickings to be had from trash cans.

Koala

Phascolarctos cinereus

The koala's name comes from an Aborigine word that means "the one who does not drink." This is quite true, as koalas live in eucalyptus trees and the succulent leaves give them all the moisture they need. This restricted diet causes them to smell strongly of eucalyptus.

Koalas are sometimes called koala bears. They are not, however, real bears but pouched mammals, related to kangaroos and opossums. In spite of their unathletic shape, koalas are good climbers, with strong, grasping toes on both hands and feet. They are less agile on the ground, but occasionally descend to eat gravelly earth, which apparently helps their digestion.

A baby koala is about an inch long at birth, but is strong enough to scramble into its mother's pouch. There it stays, feeding on milk in warmth and safety for the next seven months. When it does finally emerge, it is still far from being independent and remains with its mother, often riding on her back, for another two years.

At one time, koalas were quite common in parts of eastern Australia. Now—because of destruction of the forests, disease, and hunting in the past—they are far rarer, but careful protection in recent years has led to an increase in their numbers.

Striped skunk
Mephitis mephitis

The striped skunk hunts mainly at night, seeking the insects, rodents, and other small animals that are its food. In the daytime, it retreats to an underground den. Skunks generally live alone, but during the winter as many as ten females might huddle together for extra warmth. (Skunks are not true hibernators, although they can live on their fat for up to three months.) Often a male rests with the females and will mate with them when the weather warms up in spring. There may be as many as eight kittens in the litter. The babies grow quickly and are active after three weeks, but their mother still takes great care of them and for safety's sake often moves them from one den to another.

Although it is not very large and moves at a leisurely pace, the skunk is generally respected by other hunters. This is because its stark black-and-white fur signals that the skunk is an animal well able to protect itself. Any other inhabitant of the woods that forgets this, or does not know, is quickly reminded. First, the skunk flicks its tail upright. If this warning goes unheeded, the skunk drums loudly on the ground with its front feet. If the attacker persists, the skunk then does a handstand, swinging its body and tail over its head and producing two fine jets of an evil-smelling, oily secretion from glands below its tail. The jets can be directed accurately over 6 feet and the smell can carry more than 2 miles downwind. The stench is difficult to get rid of and no animals like it, so they keep their distance.

European badger
Meles meles

Badgers are social animals, with up to twelve living together in a sett, which is a complex of burrows usually dug into the side of a well-drained slope. Badger cubs are born in the depths of winter, and though at first they are tiny and hairless, they do not suffer from cold, because their underground nursery is snugly lined with dry grass and leaves. In mid-April they venture above ground for the first time, and within a few nights they have gained enough confidence to explore farther afield and to play rough-and-tumble games together.

Badgers have poor eyesight and live in a world of smells. They mark familiar objects with a musky scent from glands under their tails, and even very young badgers mark sticks (or each other) as they play. When they are older and have to travel around in search of food, they leave a scent trail, which probably helps them to find their way home.

A badger will eat almost anything it can find on or under the ground. Using its long claws, a hunting badger might dig up a nest of young mice or rabbits, but its main food is worms, and it can eat several hundred of these in a single night. When there are no worms, badgers eat fruit or leaves, and in spring they dig up blue-bell bulbs or the starchy roots of wild arum. During the summer months they grow fat on such food. Badgers do not hibernate in winter, but if the weather is bad they can live off their fat, and often do not bother to leave the warmth of their sett.

Gray squirrel
Sciurus carolinensis

Big nests of twigs, lodged against the trunks of woodland trees, are the homes of squirrels. These nests are used as winter resting places and as nurseries in which the young are born in spring. In the summer, squirrels retreat to more lightweight nests made of leafy twigs, in the outer branches. Baby squirrels do not stay with their mothers for long. By the time they are four months old they have left her and are looking for a place where they can find food and shelter for the winter.

Squirrels are very much at home in the trees. They can leap from one to another and run safely along branches, their long claws digging firmly into the bark. They can even go up or down a tree trunk headfirst. Squirrels also get most of their food from trees: nuts, leaves, flowers, and sappy bark, as well as insects and, if they can find them, birds' eggs or even young birds.

Squirrels are almost equally at ease on the ground, where they often hunt for fungi and dig for the roots of plants. If they are chased by a hunter such as a dog or fox, they leap away with a flick of the tail, traveling at speeds of up to 18 mph until they can reach the trees again.

As they do not hibernate, squirrels need to eat as much as they can in the autumn. When they have plenty of food, they bury the surplus. They are unable to remember where they hid it, but they can always locate it by smell. In cold weather, squirrels snooze in their nests, coming out during the day to look for the food stores they made when times were easier.

Green woodpecker
Picus viridis

In spring, the green woodpecker announces its presence in the woodlands by making a loud, laughing call. The bird is also easy to recognize as it does not perch on the branches but flies under them to land vertically on the trunk. It can do this because it is a climbing bird, having toes that spread wide to grasp the rough bark. Its tail, formed of especially stiff feathers, is used as a prop against the tree trunk.

The green woodpecker's nest is a hole that it chisels into the wood of a rotten tree. Hidden deep in the hole, the woodpecker's white eggs cannot be seen by enemies, and when the young hatch it may be this sense of security that makes them noisier than most chicks. The parents are kept busy feeding their five or six clamorous young. Sometimes the adult birds look for insects lurking in the tree bark, but mostly they feed on ants that they find on the ground. A foraging bird tears holes in the ants' nest, then licks up the insects as they run out to protect their home. The green woodpecker's tongue is sticky and extremely long—five times as long as its beak. The adult bird swallows enough ants to feed all its young each time it returns to the nest. By the time they finally fly from their nest hole, a single brood of green woodpeckers might have eaten more than a million ants.

Hazel dormouse
Muscardinus avellanarius

The hazel dormouse lives in woods where there are thickets of hazel trees and other shrubby plants. But the little animal is difficult to see, as it spends much of its time fast asleep, a habit that explains its name: Dormouse means "sleep mouse." It rests in a warm, oval-shaped nest that is usually made of the shredded bark of honeysuckle. Here, at the start of the winter, it curls up into a furry ball, its tail wrapped around its body and paws tucked under its chin, and drops into the deep sleep of hibernation, which usually lasts until spring is well under way. In the summer, it sleeps through the day in a nest that is often several feet above the ground. At night it ventures out, its large eyes and long whiskers helping it to locate nuts, berries, and insects. In spite of its plump shape, the hazel dormouse climbs with agility, clinging tightly with its paws and using its tail for balance.

Baby dormice are born early in summer. Like many climbing animals, they do not come out of their nursery nest until they are quite well grown. Even after they have left their parents, they often stay near the place where they were born. During their first summer, the youngsters work hard searching for food, because it is important that they should be as fat as possible before they begin the long fast of hibernation. It is in the second summer that their gray coats develop into the rich marmalade color of fully grown adults.

Pine marten
Martes martes

The pine marten is a tree weasel living mainly in coniferous forests and mixed woodland. Like most other members of the weasel family, it has a long, lithe body and short legs. But unlike the others, it has huge flexible feet with sharp claws that enable it to hold on to the twigs and boughs of trees so well that it is as much at home in the forest canopy as it is on the ground. Pine martens are so agile that they can even catch squirrels as they leap among the branches. They also eat mice and small ground-dwelling animals, such as voles and rabbits, and are fond of seeds and fruit, especially raspberries.

Pine martens make their dens in hollow trees and old birds' nests, but nurseries are most often at ground level, among rocks. The cubs are blind and helpless at birth and do not emerge from the den until they are eight weeks old. Despite their parents' skill and grace as climbers, the babies seem at first to be afraid of heights, although once this early reluctance is overcome they soon learn that they are safe among the branches. They even go headfirst down the trunk of a tree, and if they do fall they can usually right themselves, like cats. By the end of the summer they are the size and weight of their parents, and they leave the den where they were born, often traveling a great distance before finding a living place of their own. While foxes are among their few natural enemies, pine martens have been more seriously threatened by human hunters, who value their beautiful fur.

SEAS AND RIVERS

About seventy percent of the earth's surface is covered with water. Most of it is salt water in the oceans; only about two percent is fresh, found in rivers, lakes, ponds, and swamps. Many plants grow in water. In shallow ponds and on the margins of oceans, plants can take root. But in deep oceans and lakes, where light cannot penetrate, plants are usually minute and float near the surface. These do not have leaves or flowers but, like familiar land plants, they form the basis of the web of animal life.

There are many advantages for animals living in water. Firstly, they can range widely through the depths of their habitat. Although most animals live in the upper, light zones, there is some food and life at all depths. A second advantage is that water is dense—about 800 times as dense as air. This means that, although it prevents much speedy movement, it can act as a support. A jellyfish would simply collapse on dry land. Water also supports large animals with heavy bodies, such as whales and seals. There are no storms below the surface and, because water acts as a buffer to climate, the extremes of heat and cold found on land are unknown in the sea. Perhaps because the sea gives so uniform a living place, comparatively few kinds of animals live there, though they are often found over vast areas. By contrast, those that live in rivers, lakes, and ponds may occur only in tiny areas where conditions are especially suitable for them.

Sperm whale
Physeter catodon

The newborn sperm whale is one of the world's largest babies—about 12 feet long and weighing about 1 ton. Like all whales, it is born tail first and is able to swim alongside its mother when it is only a few minutes old. To help it feed, she pumps jets of rich milk into its throat. The baby grows quickly, but it does not take solid food for at least two more years. During this time it swims in a group totaling about forty mothers and young. These females are old friends, remaining together over many years, but when the young one is weaned it leaves to join other young whales. A female may produce her first baby when she is only ten years old, but a male is not always able to fight his way to the status of a breeding bull until he is twenty-five.

As with all whales, the sperm whales are intelligent and social. They make many sorts of sounds, some of which can be heard through several miles of water. Apart from the sounds it makes to find food by echolocation, each sperm whale makes a particular sequence of clicking noises to greet other whales. It is as though the whales announce their names, as they are often out of sight of each other.

Sperm whales swim fairly slowly, at about 6 mph, but they are capable of diving deeper than other whales—to a mile and a half or more. They feed on fish, including some sharks, but mainly on large squid, which they catch in the dark, cold depths of the ocean. Sperm whales themselves have been hunted for more than 250 years, but the recent ban on whaling could mean that they will be far less harassed in the future.

Beaver
Castor fiber

Beavers are slow moving and ungainly on land. Only in water are they quick and graceful, and only in water are they safe from their enemies. So beavers build dams that hold back stream water to form placid lakes in which they can swim. Whole families, sometimes over several generations, help to build and maintain the dam. They begin by rolling stones and mud to block part of the river. Then they add sticks and brushwood and more mud, until finally they have a strong barrier. They often also build a living place or lodge that stands above the water level, with underwater entrances by which the beavers can come and go unseen. The walls of the lodge are often several feet thick, and the floor is carpeted with dry vegetation.

Winter food of bark and twigs is stored in the lodge and there, too, the young are born, fur-covered and with their eyes open. They grow slowly, feeding on their mother's milk for up to three months, and they stay with their parents for two years. Beavers are among the few animals whose family group includes offspring of two generations living peacefully together.

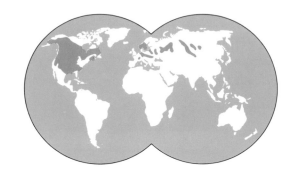

42

Nile crocodile
Crocodylus niloticus

Nile crocodiles are devoted parents, remaining together after courtship and mating. The male patrols his territory and protects his mate while she digs a pit by the water and lays up to ninety eggs. She covers the eggs with sand and vegetation and stays nearby for the next four months, not leaving even to feed. When the eggs are ready to hatch, the baby crocodiles call to their mother and, as she hears their tiny piping voices, she digs away the nest covering. The babies cut open their eggshells, using the "egg tooth" on the tip of the snout, and their mother takes them gently into a special pouch in her mouth. She carries them to shallow water and releases them, making many journeys until all the babies are safe. Then, leaving no clue for a predator, she eats the remains of the eggshells. The baby crocodiles stay near their mother for several weeks, during which time they learn to catch insects, then crabs, fish, and rodents. Upon reaching adulthood, they prey on large mammals that come to the water to drink. As crocodiles do not need to eat every day, they lead leisurely lives and enjoy basking in the sun.

Polar bear
Thalarctos maritimus

Polar bear cubs are born in the depths of the Arctic winter, in a den insulated from the bitter cold by a thick layer of snow. Compared with their mother, they are among the smallest of babies, barely bigger than guinea pigs, while she might weigh as much as 400 lbs. For the first three months the cubs remain cuddled up to her. She, for most of this time, is deeply asleep although not truly hibernating. Despite this, the cubs can suckle, and by spring, when they leave the den, their eyes are open and they are fat and well furred. Usually two or three cubs are born in a litter. Like all young carnivores, they are very playful. They wrestle and slide in the snow and gambol in the icy water, able to swim from an early age. But in these games, cubs learn skills they will need as solitary adults. The cubs remain with their mother for about two years, by which time, although they are not yet fully grown, they are capable of hunting the seals that are their chief prey.

Walrus
Odobenus rosmarus

Walruses are born early in the Arctic summer. At first they are covered with scanty reddish hair, which they lose as they grow older and their skin and blubber become thicker. A baby can swim from the day it is born and, while it is still young, may ride on its mother's shoulders as she swims speedily or dives in the sea for food.

The young one stays with its mother for the first two years of its life. It suckles her milk for at least the first year, and she protects it at all times. Polar bears are the only animals likely to attack a walrus, but other walruses, especially large males with long tusks, also pose a threat. They use their tusks in displays of aggression and, although animals of near-equal strength are rarely hurt, a defenseless young one can be. The tusks, which are hugely enlarged canine teeth, have other uses, including breaking through winter ice and enabling the animal to haul itself out of the water. A mother helps her baby with these tasks before its tusks have grown.

Great white shark
Carcharodon carcharias

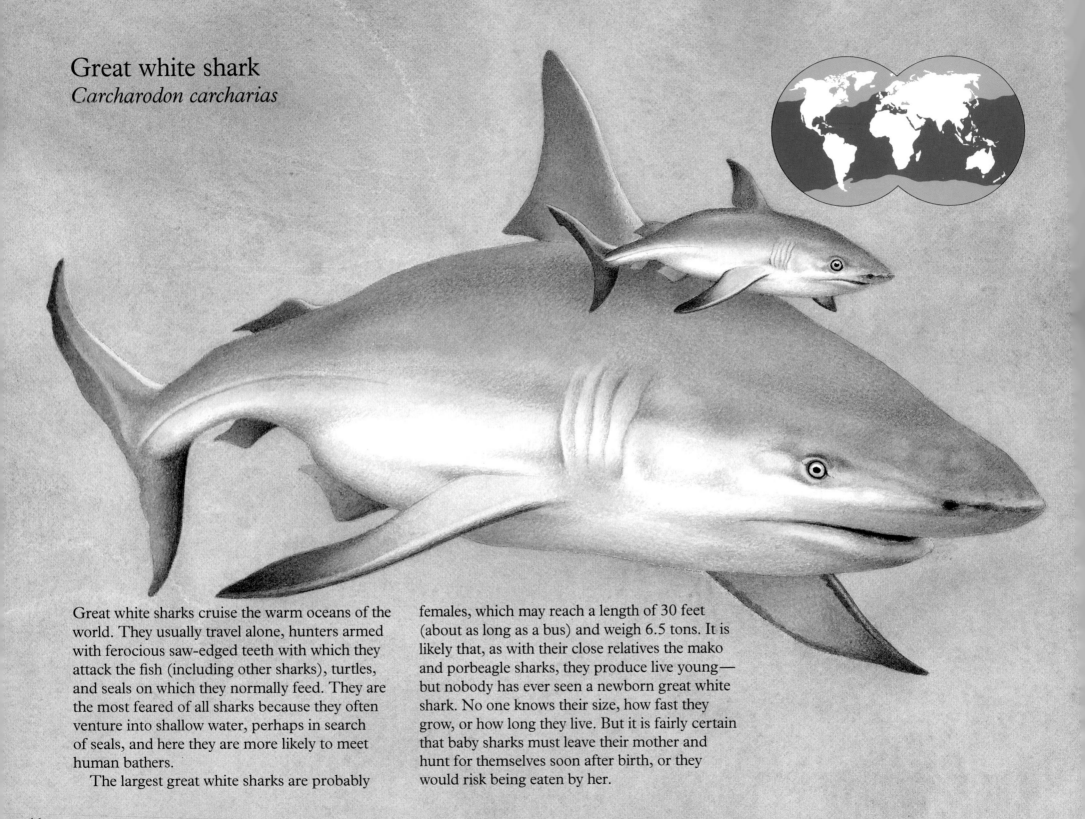

Great white sharks cruise the warm oceans of the world. They usually travel alone, hunters armed with ferocious saw-edged teeth with which they attack the fish (including other sharks), turtles, and seals on which they normally feed. They are the most feared of all sharks because they often venture into shallow water, perhaps in search of seals, and here they are more likely to meet human bathers.

The largest great white sharks are probably females, which may reach a length of 30 feet (about as long as a bus) and weigh 6.5 tons. It is likely that, as with their close relatives the mako and porbeagle sharks, they produce live young—but nobody has ever seen a newborn great white shark. No one knows their size, how fast they grow, or how long they live. But it is fairly certain that baby sharks must leave their mother and hunt for themselves soon after birth, or they would risk being eaten by her.

Green turtle
Chelonia mydas

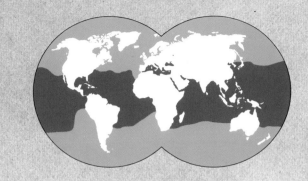

A baby green turtle could fit into the palm of a child's hand, yet its mother is well over a yard in length and as heavy as three fully grown men. Every year, green turtles migrate great distances—sometimes more than 1,500 miles—to lay their eggs on certain beaches on remote tropical islands. The females leave the water at night and crawl up the beach beyond the high-tide mark. Here, each one digs a nest hole and lays about 100 leathery-shelled eggs, which are as big as large hens' eggs. Then, after covering and hiding the eggs with sand, the females return to the sea. About two months later, the eggs begin to hatch and the baby turtles struggle to the surface. Using their flippers like little legs, they scuttle toward the sea. They must travel fast because hungry seabirds swoop over the beach ready to snap them up, and many do not survive this first short journey. The successful ones are often those that have hatched and traveled at night. Once in the water, they make for the open ocean. Now danger comes from sharks and other fish.

Baby green turtles are themselves hunters, snatching up shrimps and tiny fish, although as they grow they move to shallower areas and feed on plants. Only a few will survive to become adults, and the females will go back to the beach where they were born to lay their own eggs in turn.

Emperor penguin
Aptenodytes forsteri

Emperor penguins spend most of their lives at sea in the freezing waters of the Antarctic, but they must come ashore to produce their young. Instead of doing their courting and rearing their families in spring or summer, emperors mate and care for their eggs and chicks through the bitterest cold and darkness of the southern winter.

The parent birds come ashore at one of a small number of breeding rookeries on the ice that forms around the Antarctic continent. After courting and mating, each female lays one large egg, then returns to the sea. Her mate takes the egg and holds it on his feet, covering it with a flap of feathery skin to keep it warm. For more than two months, in intense cold and gale-force winds, he protects the egg, huddled against the other males for warmth. When the chick hatches, the male secretes a special substance for its first meal, although, as he has not fed since he left the sea, he has lost nearly half his normal body weight. Very soon after this, the females return to the colony to care for the chicks over the next forty days, and the males have their chance to feed. As the chicks grow, both parents are kept busy supplying them with food. The babies crowd together, yet each knows its own parents and follows them to be fed. By early summer the chicks have molted their thick downy coats and grown their first waterproof feathers. Then they leave the rookery for the open sea, not returning to land again for perhaps another five years.

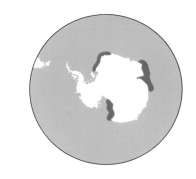

Bottle-nosed dolphin
Tursiops truncatus

In spite of its fishlike appearance and the fact that it spends all its life in water, a dolphin is a mammal, air-breathing and warm-blooded. Like other mammals, dolphins produce live young. Baby bottle-nosed dolphins come into their watery world tail first. This is a precaution against a difficult birth, as a dolphin born the same way as most mammals (headfirst) would drown before it could draw its first breath. A female dolphin about to give birth is usually accompanied by another "midwife" dolphin. She helps to push the baby to the surface of the water so that it can take its first gasp of air as soon as it is clear of its mother's body.

It is unusual for twins to be born, because dolphins have very large babies measuring about one-third their mother's length at birth. Normally, a baby keeps close to its mother, who suckles it on her rich milk for at least a year, although it may try to catch fish from the age of about six months. By the time that it is two years old, its mother will probably have another baby to care for and the young dolphin must become an independent member of the school.

For communication, dolphins rely greatly on sound, using a wide range of clicks and whistles for locating objects in the water, including their food and each other. In captivity they are also clever mimics, capable of learning long sequences of sounds as well as complex tasks.

Gray seal
Halichoerus grypus

Female gray seals desert the sea shortly before giving birth. They haul themselves ashore on rocky beaches and struggle up beyond the tide level—a difficult feat, since their hind legs have evolved into backward-turned flippers, fine for swimming but impossible to put weight on. Male seals are also present, but they are busy establishing their territories and do not interfere with the females.

At birth the gray seal pup's coat of soft, creamy-white fur looks several sizes too big for it. But its mother's milk is more than fifty percent fat and, before it is three weeks old, the little seal, which is fed four or five times a day, will have tripled its weight and filled its skin until it resembles a furry barrel. It does not increase much in length, but its food is transformed into a thick layer of blubber below the skin. At this stage, the baby's mother leaves it and, so far as is known, would not recognise it again. The pup loses its white fur, which is not properly waterproof, and develops its first seagoing coat. Soon after this, it strikes out from the coast. It sheds a little weight, but the blubber is sufficient to protect it against cold and hunger while it learns the art of catching its food— fish, crustaceans, squid, and octopus. A gray seal will be five or six years old before it is grown-up and returns to the same beach to give birth to its own young.

Bullfrog
Rana catasbaena

The deep call of the bullfrog is heard later than the trills of most of its relatives, as this giant among frogs does not usually start to breed until May or June. Then, at night, the croaking "jug-o'-rum, jug-o'-rum" rings out three or four times, to be repeated after several minutes' silence. Female bullfrogs sing also, but not as loudly as their mates.

Bullfrogs live in large pools where there is deep water and plenty of cover, as well as in shallows where food can be found among weeds. They rarely leave the water, except after heavy rain, when they may travel overland to another pond. The females lay between 10,000 and 20,000 eggs. These hatch in a few days and, as with other frogs, the tadpoles feed at first on minute water plants. They are the target for voracious animals such as water beetles, but if they escape with their lives, even a badly damaged tail can be regrown. As they mature, their diet includes small animals. Bullfrog tadpoles develop more slowly than the young of most other frogs, and take at least two years to become adults.

Adult bullfrogs eat a wide range of animal food, including worms, snails, and grubs that they catch in the water. They also eat small fish and even little snakes and turtles, if they can catch them. On the muddy edge of the water they might even snatch small birds. When the frog makes its capture, it hops back into the water to swallow it. The frogs are themselves food for many predators: herons, otters, mink—and people, who find their massive hind legs to be good eating.

Common teal

Anas crecca

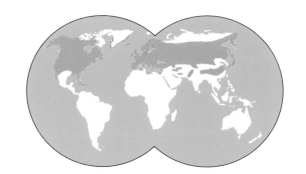

The handsome male teal plays no part in caring for his family. His less brightly colored mate chooses the site for her nest, usually somewhere not far from fresh water but protected by shrubs or other vegetation. She makes the nest in a small hollow, lining it with leaves and down from her body. When she has laid eight or more cream-colored eggs, she settles down to incubate them for over three weeks. She leaves them only briefly to drink or feed, first covering them with down to camouflage them and keep them warm.

As soon as the baby teal hatch they are able to leave the nest and start looking for food. To begin with, they venture onto the water only as darkness falls. They grow quickly on a diet of tiny snails, insects, and worms that they find in and around the water. By the time that they are a month old they can fly, and they leave their mother to join the flocks of adult birds.

In winter many teal migrate from northern lands where the surface water is frozen. Some go as far south as Africa, but most remain in temperate areas, on ponds, slow-flowing streams, or estuaries. Any unusual sight sends the flock springing into the air and flying low and fast to a safer place.

GRASSLANDS

The prairies of North America, the steppes of eastern Europe and central Asia, the pampas of South America, the savannas of Africa, and much of Australia are areas in which grasses and other herbaceous plants flourish. Trees may grow by rivers or where there is underground water, but in general there is too little rainfall, and grasslands form open, windy plains—hot in summer and, in the prairies and steppes, very cold in winter.

Grasses differ from other plants in that their growing point is low down, not at the top of a shoot, so the plant can be cropped by grazing animals and yet continue to grow. In the past, grazing animals dominated the landscape— bison in North America, wild horses on the steppes, and kangaroos in Australia. Only in parts of Africa, however, do large numbers of grazing animals remain—antelopes and zebras and the carnivores that prey on them. Elsewhere, man has taken over grasslands, either for sheep and cattle, or for growing grain.

Other life used to thrive beneath the surface. Small burrowing animals, such as the prairie dogs of North America and the marmots and susliks of the steppes, lived in huge "townships" of over a million animals. They fed mainly on grasses and often scattered the seeds that ensured fresh growth. Their burrowing acted as a plow in turning over fresh soil. Small carnivores, including ferrets and snakes, hunted the burrowers. Most of these animals have also disappeared, although many insects of the open plains have managed to survive.

Giraffe
Giraffa camelopardalis

The baby giraffe arrives in the world with a bump, as its mother gives birth standing up and the young one drops to the ground—always, it seems, without hurting itself. It is a large baby—as heavy as a young man, and taller. Soon it scrambles up on wobbly legs to take its first meal of milk, and in a few days it begins to nibble leaves. Before it is a week old, it joins the other babies of the herd, who spend most of their time playing together while their mothers feed.

Young giraffes grow fast, but do not reach their full height until they are five to seven years old. Females are slightly smaller than their mates. A big male can stretch his neck 18 feet into the trees to gather food. Giraffes have extraordinarily long tongues, which enable them to pull off the tender leaves and shoots growing on thorny shrubs such as acacia. But when it comes to drinking, the giraffe's height is a disadvantage.

The members of a herd may scatter over as much as a mile, but their good eyesight keeps them in touch and their ability to run fast means that they can act as a group if need be. Baby giraffes are sometimes caught by lions, but adults can generally defend themselves against all natural enemies by kicking out strongly. Compared to most other animals, giraffes lead peaceable lives. Males engage in gentle wrestling matches with their necks, but real fights are rare.

Cheetah
Acinonyx jubatus

A cheetah mother seems to be nervous for the safety of her young cubs. Although she usually chooses a well-hidden den, she is likely to move the babies to a new nursery several times in their first few weeks. The father plays no part in the cubs' upbringing, but their mother spends every night with them, feeding and cleaning them. She leaves early in the day to hunt, returning after she has made a kill.

The cubs grow quickly and become very playful, stalking and chasing in mock hunts. At the age of six weeks, they begin to follow their mother, and although they are not yet weaned, they try to eat meat. Soon afterward, the mother teaches her cubs how to make a kill. Sometimes she captures a young animal and takes it to them, retrieving it if it escapes their inexpert attention. They learn the cheetah method of dispatching prey, which is to knock it off balance, then throttle it. Later, they discover the art of selecting prey of the right size—young cheetahs often tackle animals that are far too big and heavy for them. They find out the best way of stalking and the distance at which they must start their final run. An adult cheetah, as it closes in on its quarry, is the fastest moving animal in the world and can reach a speed of 60 mph. Although cheetahs range over large parts of Africa, they are rare in the south and west.

Impala
Aepyceros melampus

Impala herds are on the move through much of the year, although they do not generally travel great distances. When impala are alarmed by an enemy, such as a lion, they leap away in all directions. It is as though the whole herd explodes into a blur of flying hooves, bodies, and horns. Even young impala may be part of the apparent panic, which probably serves to confuse the predator at a time when a moment's hesitation can cost it a meal.

A mother impala gives birth to her fawn in a sheltered spot away from the main herd. She remains with it for several days, then leads it to meet the rest of the group. Fawns keep together, though each one knows its own mother and goes to her to be fed. Young impala begin to nibble at leaves when they are about four weeks old. When they are weaned, the young females stay with the herd but young males are driven away. They join others to form nonterritorial bachelor groups. As they grow older and stronger they eventually achieve a territory, and with it the right to mate and have fawns of their own.

Great Indian rhinoceros
Rhinoceros unicornis

Great Indian rhinoceroses never move far from water, as they need to drink every day and they like to bathe and wallow frequently. They usually live alone, although sometimes several gather at a favorite mud hole. They are most active in the mornings and evenings, when they feed on grass, water plants, and the twigs of shrubs and trees.

Indian rhinos can be surprisingly active and fast moving, and courting animals sometimes chase each other at high speed. The young are born in March and April. The single baby is large and well developed and able to walk soon after birth. Unlike their African relatives, Indian rhinos are not aggressive. A cow may charge in defense of her calf, but if she attacks she uses her sharp teeth instead of her horn, which is rather short and blunt. Rhinos have poor eyesight and rely mostly on their acute sense of smell to warn them of danger.

Not long ago, these large animals ranged over much of northern India. Now, as a result of the destruction of their living places, and of poaching, only about 1,000 of them survive. Most of these live in reserves.

American bison
Bison bison

At one time the North American bison was the most abundant large animal in the world. More than fifty million lived on the prairies and in woodland and upland areas where they could get enough grass to eat. Yet within a few hundred years of the discovery of America, they had been almost exterminated. By 1890, fewer than 1,000 remained. Now, with strict conservation, the numbers have risen to about 50,000, almost all of which are descended from captive animals.

Present day herds are formed of groups of females, and calves up to the age of three years. The males live in smaller groups, or alone. They join the females in late summer, which is the time of the rut, or breeding season. Then the males fight in head-butting trials of strength, and if one wins a mate, he prevents others from approaching her for several days. The calves are born in late spring or early summer. They are large and active and within a few hours of birth are able to run around. Although it suckles only for about seven months, the calf remains with its mother long after weaning.

Bison are active during the day, moving about in a small area as they graze across the plains. They often use mud wallows or dust baths or rub against trees or boulders, probably to combat the many parasites that live in their fur.

Lion
Panthera leo

A newborn lion cub usually has three or four brothers and sisters of the same age. At first, their mother hides them in safety, but when they are a few weeks old she takes them to join her family group, or "pride." As a rule, all the lionesses in a pride are closely related—often they are sisters—so cubs belong to a big family, with lots of playmates for games of tag and pounce. When they are hungry, their aunts feed them on milk if their own mother is away.

The lions help to keep the cubs' world safe by patrolling and guarding the large area in which the pride lives, although the lionesses do most of the work of hunting. The cubs feed on milk until they are about seven months old, but even when they are quite tiny they follow their mothers and begin to learn how to stalk and catch their prey. They do not help in the hunt until they are about a year old and cannot make a kill for themselves until at least three months after this. When they grow up, female cubs remain in the same pride as their mothers. The young males wander off and, after several years, when they are fully grown and strong, they may find a family group of their own.

Hippopotamus
Hippopotamus amphibius

Hippopotamus means "water horse," and although a hippo is nothing like a horse, it does spend most of its life in the warm, shallow waters of rivers and lakes. A baby hippo can swim before it can walk, and in a stream or reed bed where crocodiles might be a threat, it often scrambles up onto its mother's broad back for complete safety. Hippos swim and dive gracefully and can even walk on the riverbed. They can close their ears and nostrils and stay submerged for up to half an hour; or they can float with just eyes and nose above water. But on land, where hippos go at night to feed on grass and other tender plants, their bulk makes them awkward animals. Female hippos and their young usually live in peaceful groups. But males are aggressive, driving other males away by showing their huge, sharp front teeth.

Plains zebra
Equus burchelli

Every zebra has a different pattern of stripes. These act as identification marks, as zebras live in family groups of about a dozen animals. Each zebra knows all the others and recognizes them, even from a distance. A herd of 10,000 zebras has hundreds of such groups and, although the herd may be migrating, the families keep their positions in relation to one another. Every day the lead stallion of each family checks that all is well by visiting and greeting the stallions of other groups. He may make as many as thirty such visits in a single day.

A zebra foal is brought into the family group soon after it is born, but for the first few days the mare prevents the others from having close contact with it. After this, it begins to walk and play with the other young zebras. The mother feeds and grooms her foal and it, in turn, nibbles at her coat. It is thought that mutual grooming of this sort is the basis of the strong affection that exists between members of a zebra group. At about two years of age, a filly foal is grown-up and leaves her family. She may join several other groups briefly before settling down with the stallion with whom she will probably spend the rest of her life. Colt foals remain with the group, even after they are mature. They often seem to have a special bond of friendship with their fathers, though they do eventually leave, sometimes to join a bachelor group of young males, and finally to become the lead stallions of families of their own.

Ostrich
Struthio camelus

In the breeding season, a male ostrich attracts females with a loud, roaring call. One female, the "major" hen, chooses a scrape he has made in the ground and lays her eggs. These are added to by other, "minor" hens. Eventually there might be over thirty eggs in the nest—far too many to incubate—so the major hen pushes some out, probably to be eaten by vultures or jackals. For six weeks, the female sits on the nest during the day and the male sits at night, until the eggs hatch. The chicks can feed themselves from the day of birth, and if in danger they flatten themselves on the ground, where they are difficult to see, while the adults display their plumage to distract the predator. Month-old chicks can run from the danger at a speed of 25 mph. At a year, they are nearly as tall as their parents, though they will not become parents for another two or three years.

Gray kangaroo
Macropus giganteus

The gray kangaroo lives among trees, although it feeds mainly on grasses that grow in open spaces. Kangaroos spend much of the day resting and begin to feed late in the afternoon. They are wary animals and leap away at tremendous speed if they are frightened. They have been recorded as traveling at 25 mph. The greatest distance covered in a single bound is 40 feet.

A group or "mob" of between ten and twenty females and their young usually live together. They are joined by males only when they are ready to mate. Gray kangaroos are mostly born in summer, when food is plentiful. At birth, a baby is about as big as the tip of a human finger and weighs about one thirtieth of an ounce. Despite its tiny size, it has well-developed, clawed front limbs. It scrambles quickly through its mother's fur to her pouch, where it attaches itself to a nipple. At first, the mother pumps milk into the baby's mouth, as it is too feeble to suck. The baby, which is called a joey, does not leave the pouch for nine months, and for another six weeks it returns there regularly. Almost as soon as the joey is independent, the female kangaroo produces another baby.

67

Rabbit
Oryctolagus cuniculus

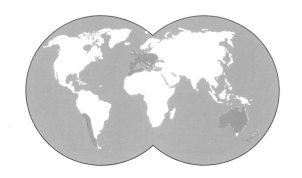

The European rabbit probably lived originally only in Spain and North Africa. Although it has been taken to many other parts of the world, the animal still has many habits that remind us that it originated in hot, dry countries. Rabbits hate wet weather, for instance, and shake the dew from their paws if they have to run through damp grass.

Usually, a great many rabbits live together in a complex of tunnels and runs called a warren. The older, dominant bucks and does occupy the central area, protected by outlying, lower-ranking members of the group. In the early part of the year the does make short burrows that they line with dry grass and fur pulled from their own undersides. These are the nurseries in which baby rabbits are born. There are almost always five young in the family. At first the babies are blind and helpless but they grow quickly, and in about twenty days are ready to explore the world outside. They eat many kinds of plants, both wild and cultivated. Wherever rabbits are, their senses of sight, smell, and hearing are constantly alert to danger of any kind.

Jack rabbit
Lepus californicus

All rabbits and their relatives have long ears, but those of the jack rabbit are biggest of all. Hearing is the most important sense it uses in its constant battle for survival.

Jack rabbits usually feed at night, and during the day lie hidden under a bush or in a small scrape on the ground. If a carnivore, such as a coyote or a large hawk, comes close, the jack rabbit leaps up and bounds away. It zigzags bewilderingly, sometimes leaping high so that it can see its enemy's progress. As it runs, it keeps its huge ears folded back, as spiny plants could injure their delicate tissue.

Despite its name, the jack rabbit is really a hare. Like other hares, female jacks produce leverets, which are open-eyed and well furred at birth. They lie in a scrape, or "form," waiting for their mother to come and feed them at night. But this stage of their life is quickly over, and they soon disperse to live alone. Their mother will probably have several more litters during the year, but many baby jack rabbits do not survive to adulthood, as it is the young and inexperienced that often fall prey to enemies.

Harvest mouse
Micromys minutus

The name *harvest mouse* suggests an animal that lives in grain fields. While this was true when crops were cut by hand, the use of modern farm machinery means that the harvest mouse cannot survive in such places, although they are still found in areas of tall, coarse grasses.

Harvest mice climb well, using their prehensile tails to steady and support themselves. They build their summer nests early in the season among tall grasses. They strip the long thin leaves of living plants into even narrower ribbons and use these to make the scaffolding of the nest by weaving them around the stems of several other plants. When this is strong enough, it is lined with more grass to make a snug nursery. There is no special entrance hole—the animals just push in anywhere.

Up to thirteen baby harvest mice can be born in a single litter. At first they are blind and helpless, but they are safe within the tiny nest, which is almost impossible to see. The reason for this is that the nest's outer leaves are growing and remain the same color as the surrounding plants. By the end of the summer the nest will be perhaps a foot and a half taller, as it is built near the ground and moves up as the parent plants grow. It is unlikely that the young mice notice this, for the babies develop rapidly and go their own way before they are five weeks old. When they leave, their mother gives birth to another family.

DESERTS

Deserts are areas in which less than 10 inches of rain falls in any year. They may be sandy or stony, hot like the Sahara or cold, at least in winter, like the Gobi. They are usually found in the shadow of mountains or in the interior of continents, reached only by winds that have already shed the water they once carried. Usually, rain comes in a torrential storm, and sometimes there may not be so much as a shower for several more years. As a result, deserts look, at first sight, to be nearly lifeless.

Very few large animals can live for long in deserts. Those that do often have thick coats, which act as insulation from the heat and also keep them warm when the temperature drops at night. Like camels and oryx, they survive on harsh, tough plant food and can go for long periods without drinking. All desert animals conserve body moisture: They do not sweat, they produce little urine, and even their droppings are dry. Small mammals such as mice and jerboas live in deep burrows, unaffected by the outside temperature, and are active only during the cool of the night. They feed mainly on the seeds of plants. Some get enough water from their food and from dew, and conserve it so effectively, that they do not need to drink throughout their whole lives. Small carnivores, including reptiles, can also survive long periods without feeding. Insects are found in deserts too, many living underground. Some insects and plants appear as if by magic soon after rain and are not seen again until another storm makes the apparently empty desert bloom.

Arabian oryx
Oryx leucoryx

At one time the Arabian oryx lived in the vast areas stretching from Syria and Iraq through the Arabian peninsula to Israel and Jordan. It preferred flat, gravelly plains or the edges of dunes, where many kinds of desert plants grow.

The oryx can detect from great distances places where rain has fallen, although it is also able to survive for months on end without drinking. Sometimes it digs shallow pits in soft ground, probably because such places are cooler to rest in. It is alert, wary, and keen-sighted, and in the past, hunting such animals on foot or on horseback was a test of endurance and skill.

The hunting, however, was uncontrolled, and by the beginning of this century, Arabian oryxes were to be found only in the Arabian peninsula. From there they were exterminated by oil-rich hunters in jeeps, using modern firearms. The last wild Arabian oryx was killed in 1972.

Fortunately, conservationists had foreseen the end of the species in the wild and in 1962 two males and a female were caught in the desert and taken, with six zoo oryxes, to the zoo in Phoenix, Arizona. So carefully have they been cared for and bred, that the herd now numbers over 150 animals, and within the last few years Arabian oryxes have been returned to Jordan, where they are protected in a large reserve, and to Oman, where two small herds have now been released into the wild. The animals seem to be thriving, but it will be some years before herds 100 strong, as reported in the old days, will be seen again in the deserts of the Middle East.

Fennec fox

Fennecus zerda

The tiny fennec fox waits until after dark before leaving the burrow in which it has avoided the searing heat of the day. Its huge ears enable it to hear the slightest movement made by the lizards or insects on which it feeds, and it can leap to catch a desert bird disturbed from its nest and return to eat the eggs or chicks.When there are locust swarms, the fennec feeds well; at other times it may turn to plant food.

For much of the time, fennec foxes live in small colonies, but as the breeding season approaches, the males become agressive and begin to mark out territories for themselves and their mates. The cubs, usually three in a litter, sometimes as many as five, are born in later winter or early spring. When they are very young, their father does not enter the burrow in which the vixen cares for them, although he stays in the area. The cubs are suckled for over two months before they are fully weaned, and even after that they probably continue to live near their parents.

The fennec has few enemies other than man, but if pursued it can run easily, even over shifting sand, as its feet are covered with hairs that provide a grip on the unstable surface. And when it comes to a suitable hiding place, the fennec fox can dig so fast that it seems to disappear underground as if by magic.

Arabian camel
Camelus dromedarius

No one knows exactly what wild Arabian, or one-humped, camels looked like or how they behaved, as this hot-desert species has been extinct as a wild animal for centuries. But we can make a good guess, since domesticated Arabian camels, or dromedaries, have been released in several dry parts of the world, including the Southwest of the United States and central Australia. Nearer to their original home, in the Sahara, camels left to their own devices probably behave much like their wild ancestors. They seem to live in parties that include bachelor groups of males, nursery groups of females with their newborn young, and groups of females with calves up to two years old. The calves are usually born in the spring months. The babies are large and well developed, and able to walk on their day of birth. But they are not completely independent until they are four years old, and even then they are not fully grown.

A camel is able to carry heavy loads across waterless lands, as it can go without drinking for long periods and conserves moisture in its body. It does not carry water in its hump, which is made up mainly of fatty tissue. Over a period of time, a camel does lose water, but it can stand a higher degree of dehydration than other animals. It can survive a water loss equal to over forty percent of its weight (about ten percent is fatal to man) but it must recover this quickly, so when it reaches water it drinks deeply. One camel is recorded to have drunk over 60 quarts at a time.

Bactrian camel
Camelus bactrianus

Bactrian (two-humped) camels were domesticated much later than their one-humped relatives, and sizeable populations survived in the drier parts of northeastern Asia until the 1920s. Since then, as a result of hunting and of their living places being taken over by man, the numbers of this cold-desert species have declined, and now the total world population of wild bactrian camels is thought to be about 500 animals. Although they live in herds of thirty or so, they are so shy and wary that they are difficult to approach. Their eyesight and sense of smell are excellent, and they can run across rough country at speeds of over 35 mph. Unlike most other animals, they move the fore and hind legs on the same side of the body forward together, which gives bactrian camels their characteristic rolling gait.

Like Arabian camels, bactrians conserve water by having very few sweat glands in their skin; they lose hardly any water in their droppings or urine, and not even the moisture in their breath is allowed to escape, as a groove running from the nose to the upper lip enables trapped liquid to be swallowed. Also like Arabian camels, the cold-desert species can eat almost anything that their hostile environment provides. No growth is too dry or thorny for them—they will even take salty plants—and if there is nothing else, they will eat bones or skin.

Bactrian camels are born in March and April. Twins are very rare. Like the Arabian camel, the babies are active from the day of birth.

Pallas's sandgrouse
Syrrhaptes paradoxus

Pallas's sandgrouse lives in many sorts of dry places. It likes deep, dry, dusty soil for dust bathing but avoids the drifting sands of totally waterless deserts because it must drink each day, even if that means flying many miles. The sandgrouse that live in cold deserts migrate to warmer places in spring. Sometimes they travel westward and so are occasionally seen in western Europe, although they rarely remain there for more than one season.

Pallas's sandgrouse are social birds. Large flocks often travel together, their wings making a whistling sound, which can be heard over a long distance. Yet when the flocks arrive at their breeding grounds, the pairs of birds spread out so that there may be half a mile between neighbors. Two or three eggs are laid in a small scrape in the ground and both parents share the month-long task of incubation. The newly hatched chicks can peck up the seeds of grasses and other plants that are their food, but until they learn to fly, they are dependent on their parents for water.

It is likely that Pallas's sandgrouse fetches water in the same way as closely related species. The female watches the chicks while the male flies to a watering hole in which he stands until the feathers of his underside are thoroughly soaked. Then he flies back to the chicks, who line up to drink in turn by drawing individual feathers through their beaks.

Greater roadrunner
Geococcyx californiana

The roadrunner is aptly named, for although it can fly, it rarely does so. When disturbed, it runs off at high speed. If pressed, it dodges into the chaparral, or scrub forest, of the semidesert areas where it lives, a habit that has given it the alternative name *chaparral cock*.

Roadrunners often come into contact with people, in camps or on farms. Most people are amused by their antics, such as chasing golf balls. Surely the birds do not see these as food, as their diet consists mainly of lizards and snakes, including rattlesnakes. Mice and baby rabbits are sometimes caught, and insects of many kinds,

the bird leaping high into the air to grab a grasshopper or flying cicada. If all else fails, it will seek out the fruits of the cactus.

A roadrunner builds its untidy nest of sticks in a thorny bush. The eggs are laid at intervals of two or three days and the first chick may be ready to leave the nest just as the last one is hatching. If an enemy approaches, the roadrunner remains on the nest until the last moment, then hops off and attempts to distract the intruder by limping away. When she has led the predator sufficiently far, she runs off at full speed.

The roadrunner, once a familiar bird of the American West, is becoming rare. Its original home range is often disturbed by human activity, causing the bird to retreat to wilder places.

Merriam's kangaroo rat
Dipodymys merriami

The kangaroo rat is not a kangaroo, and although it is a rodent, it is more closely related to the squirrels than to true rats. There are at least twenty kinds of kangaroo rats and they often live in areas far from water, as they are able to survive indefinitely without drinking.

Kangaroo rats are solitary animals and great burrowers, making dens in which to shelter from the heat of the day. They emerge after dark to look for seeds, leaves, and insects, moving slowly on all fours, pausing to scrabble for food, then picking up morsels with their tiny forefeet. They also store seeds underground and will fight any neighbor who dares raid their granary. If they are frightened, kangaroo rats leap away on their hind legs and, balanced by their long tails, can cover over 6 feet in a single bound.

Baby kangaroo rats born early in the spring may give birth to their own young before the summer is out. Despite their ability to breed rapidly, many kinds of kangaroo rats are now rare, though Merriam's is still quite common.

Thorny devil
Moloch horridus

The thorny devil's name conjures up a vision of a truly alarming creature, quite different from this inoffensive little lizard. Its bizarre spines are probably a defense against its enemies. Few carnivorous mammals are able to survive the heat and dryness of the thorny devil's home, but there are snakes, such as the death adder and the black snake, that depend largely on lizards for their food. The thorny devil's largest spines are on its head and—as all snakes swallow their prey whole and headfirst—positioned where they would make the hungriest snake hesitate.

The thorny devil is active during the day, when the desert temperatures are at their highest. Most animals are deterred by the heat, but this lizard is apparently at its best when its body temperature is about 98° F. It searches for ants, mopping them up on its short but sticky tongue. One thorny devil is recorded to have eaten 1,000 ants in an hour and 7,000 in a day. But, like other reptiles, the thorny devil may not be so lucky every day and can go for long periods with little food. It does get a certain amount of liquid from the bodies of its prey, but even if there are no ants, the thorny devil can still manage. Any water, such as dew, that condenses on its skin is taken by capillary action through tiny channels to the corner of the animal's mouth, a mechanism which enables the thorny devil to survive where few others can.

MOUNTAINS

High mountains are inhospitable places. The tops of the highest ranges, even on the equator, are permanently snowclad. Strong winds and rain may lash the rock faces, sweeping away all but the hardiest of living things. Yet those same rocks can bake under a glaring sun. Farther down, temperatures and winds are less extreme. Below the zone of rock and ice grow mosses and lichens; then small flowering plants, then shrubs, and finally, on the lowest slopes, dense forest. Most specialized are the alpine plants of the upper zone. Deep-rooted and slow growing, many form a "cushion" that resists the force of the wind and makes a snug haven for insects.

Mountains are often the last stronghold of flesh-eating mammals and birds, driven from milder habitats by man's activities. They include cats, such as the puma and snow leopard, and birds, such as eagles and condors. High ranges are also the home of surefooted plant-eaters like wild goats and sheep. These tend to be stockily built, with heavy coats, but even they retreat to lower levels in winter. Small mammals, such as alpine marmots, usually survive by hibernating in warm burrows.

The brilliant flowers of the high zones provide food for insects, among them many butterflies unknown in other habitats. Living highest of all are tiny scavengers such as springtails and mites, feeding mainly on pollen grains and seeds carried by the wind. Their enemies are spiders and beetles, small hunters that shelter under rocks against the extremes of their environment.

Bighorn sheep
Ovis canadensis

A bighorn lamb is born in a very secluded spot, usually on a ledge protected by an overhang, for at first it is wobbly on its feet and cannot run. Its mother stays close by, ready to repel the eagles which are its main enemy. She leaves the lamb only when she must have food or water. After about a week it is strong enough to follow her and begin to nibble grasses.

Through the summer months, mother and baby belong to a group of about ten animals, including mothers, lambs, yearlings, and two-year-olds, which are almost ready to become independent. The young ones can play on the steepest slopes, as their hooves are softer at the center of the foot than at the edge and act like suction cups, giving a grip on the rocks. Carnivores such as bobcats and coyotes stand little chance of catching bighorns, which are so much more agile.

In autumn the rams, which have been living in separate herds, seek out the females. They become quarrelsome and often fight. The rivals paw at each other with their sharp front hooves, then move a few yards apart. Suddenly they hurtle toward each other, building up a speed of about 18 mph until their heads meet with a crack that can be heard a mile away. The animals often appear dazed, if unhurt, by the force of the blow. Fights may continue intermittently for several hours, with the winner usually being the larger and heavier male.

Winter arrives soon after the mating season and the bighorns retreat to lower ground, where they feed mainly on shrubs and woody plants. Although always wary, bighorns are no match for man, who has drastically reduced their numbers.

Spectacled bear
Tremarctos ornatus

As darkness falls, spectacled bears leave their secure hiding places in upland forests in the northern Andes. They wander out to search for the fruit which forms the main part of their food, often climbing large trees to reach it. Sometimes they make a platform of broken branches high above the ground, so that they have a comfortable place where they can feed in safety and reach further supplies. When fruit is not available they use their great strength to tear the bark off certain trees so that they can get at the sweet pith beneath. They also like to eat the tender hearts of palm trees, pulling out the unopened leaves. Meat, mainly in the form of rodents and insects, forms a very small part of their diet.

Spectacled bear cubs are probably born in about July, although very few have ever been seen in the wild. As with all bears, the babies are very tiny compared with their mother: They tip the scale at only 10 oz. while she may weigh over 130 lbs. It is not known how long the young suckle or remain with their mother, but it is probably a considerable time.

Spectacled bears have often been destroyed when they have come into contact with man. Many people believe, mistakenly, that they are a danger to livestock; they are also hunted for their meat, fat, and skin. Their numbers are now far smaller, but they survive in inaccessible places, where they have been able to adapt to many types of food and living conditions.

Vicuna
Vicugna vicugna

The vicuna is said by some people to be the most graceful of hoofed animals. It is also one of the hardiest, being able to live at heights above 9,000 feet. Even in the rarefied atmosphere of such places, it can run at speeds approaching 25 mph. Usually, vicuna live in family parties, which demonstrate their association by using communal dung heaps. Each group is led by a male and includes several females and their young. They have different territories for feeding and resting. Both are defended throughout the year, but the corridor between them is left unguarded. The vicuna feeds almost entirely on grasses. Its eyesight is very good—although its senses of hearing and smell are not so important—and it keeps a sharp watch for danger while grazing.

A baby vicuna is born in February or March. It is able to stand and walk when it is fifteen minutes old but remains close to its mother, sleeping by her side for at least the first eight months and continuing to suckle for a couple of months after that. When they are about eighteen months old, the young males are driven from the group by their fathers. Females remain a little longer, but then they leave and join another family, producing their first kid when they are about three years old.

In the harsh climate of the high Andes, the vicuna's wonderfully dense and soft coat keeps it warm. In the days of the Incas, centuries ago, vicuna were rounded up and shorn, but in more recent times they have been slaughtered for their valuable wool, which has led to a drop in numbers. Today, due to careful conservation, they are beginning to increase again.

Alpine ibex
Capra ibex

Ibex are generally seen on bare, rocky mountain slopes above the treeline, at heights between 7,500 and 10,500 feet. They are marvelously surefooted animals, being able to run and jump on the steepest of slopes. During the day ibex rest, often sunbathing in sheltered spots among the crags. At night they are more active and descend to slightly lower ground to feed, mainly on shrubby upland plants and lichens. They do not venture below the treeline except in the most bitter winter weather.

Alpine ibex live in herds consisting either of males, which occupy the highest ground, or nannies and their young, which are found at slightly lower levels. Only during the rut, or mating season, which takes place in the early winter months, are they seen together. Unlike most other hoofed animals, ibex often produce twins. These are born about midsummer when there is plenty of food and reasonable weather in the heights. They are active very soon after birth and within a few days begin to nibble at solid food. Although her horns are not as large as those of her mate, the female will use them to fight off anything that menaces her kids. Despite the early activity of the young, a female ibex is unlikely to breed before she is four or five years old. As if to compensate for this late start, she may live until she is fifteen or more.

Man is the most dangerous of the ibex's enemies and, by the beginning of this century, had reduced their numbers to a very low level, the animals surviving mainly in the Alps of northern Italy. Thanks to strict conservation, ibex now number several thousand.

Andean condor
Vultur gryphus

The Andean condor is not the heaviest flying bird, nor does it have the largest wingspan, but it must rank as the most impressive, for its wing area exceeds that of any other bird. It can soar and glide for hours, controlling the air that supports it with subtle movements of the open, fingerlike primary feathers.

Andean condors may be found in upland areas at heights of over 12,000 feet, although they search for food at all levels, even on the coast. A condor's usual diet is carrion, and it scans the ground for dead or dying animals. It cannot smell even the most putrifying remains and relies on its eyesight to find food.

Before mating, the male condor performs a dramatic display, spreading the huge wings and bowing his brightly colored head in front of his mate. Condors do not make a nest, but both parents incubate the single egg, laid on a rocky ledge, and care for the chick. Its growth is rapid, but it is not capable of flight until it is six months old and stays with its parents for a further year. Andean condors are long-lived birds, possibly surviving for twenty years.

Golden eagle
Aquila chrysaetos

Golden eagles work hard to build their nests. They break small branches from trees and tug heather from the ground, producing a pile of sticks 6 feet high and more than 4.5 feet in diameter. The cup of the nest is lined with wool and grass so that the chicks have a warm and well protected nursery. Sometimes the nest is sited in a tree, but more usually it is on a ledge protected by an overhang of solid rock. Eagles, which are long-lived birds, mate for life. They may have several nest sites in their territory and return to them in different years, refurbishing them each time they are used.

Golden eagles usually lay two eggs. The female starts to incubate as soon as the first one is produced. Nearly two months later it hatches, and a few days after this the second baby bird emerges. By this time the first chick has already started to grow, and the difference in size is maintained until they are fledged, almost three months later. During this time both parents scour their huge terrirory for food. Their prey is generally animals the size of rabbits or hares, but sometimes much larger creatures are caught, such as foxes or even young roe deer. The parent birds tear at the food with their huge beaks and gently feed the young ones with scraps of a manageable size.

Long before they are able to fly, the babies stand by the nest, building up muscle by flapping their unfinished wings. When they finally launch themselves from the ledge, they can swoop and soar and watch like their parents, but they need practice before they can catch enough food for survival. They are not independent of their parents for another three months and will not have chicks for at least three years.

Giant panda
Ailuropoda melanoleuca

The giant panda is one of the world's rarest animals, with fewer than 1,000 surviving in the wild. It is also one of the world's best-known—it is appropriately the symbol of the World Wildlife Fund, with the animals totally protected by law and about sixty percent of the wild population living in twelve special reserves.

Giant pandas seem to be solitary animals, marking their territory by clawing tree trunks. They also scent-mark trees. They have forepaws with an extra "thumb," enabling them to hold the stems of umbrella bamboo, their main food. This large grass is long-lived, but dies after flowering. It is a year or so before the new plants are well grown. Scattered as they are across 11,000 sq. miles of mountainous country, at altitudes up to 12,000 feet, pandas cannot easily find new feeding areas. In one mountain area, in 1974–6, about 100 pandas died of starvation after the bamboo flowered. Unlike some animals saved from extinction, the giant panda rarely breeds successfully in zoos.

Red panda
Ailurus fulgens

Although giant and red pandas share a name, the two animals are not closely related. The giant panda is a member of the bear family, while the red panda is more similar to the raccoon.

Red pandas live in mountainous forests at heights between 5,000 and 12,000 feet. They seem to prefer lower temperatures than giant pandas do, and in China, where the two animals occur in the same region, the red panda always inhabits the higher slopes. Red pandas are often found in pairs or small family groups. During the day they sleep, sometimes hunched on branches, but more usually a red panda finds a hollow tree in which to curl up, with its bushy tail wrapped around it. It wakes as darkness begins to fall. Strangely, although it is a good climber, it finds most of its food on the ground. Red pandas are technically carnivores, but they eat a wide variety of plants, including bamboo shoots, grasses, the roots of many sorts of plants, fruits, berries, and acorns. Sometimes they dig up a nest of young rodents, or find a bird's nest with eggs or young, and occasionally they eat insects or grubs.

Little is known about the social life of red pandas, but it is very likely that they are territorial, since they mark rocks and trees with a musky scent. In zoos, young have been born in late June. The litter size is small, rarely more than two cubs, which are suckled for over four months and cared for by their mother or sometimes by both parents for at least a year before they become independent.

Facts and Figures

Distribution maps show the approximate range over which a particular animal is found and do not indicate size of population.
Figures apply to a fully grown adult unless otherwise specified.

ALPINE IBEX

Body length: c. 5 ft.
Height: 25–40 in. (male)
      c. 25 in. (female)
Weight: 175–255 lbs. (male)
      65–110 lbs. (female)

AMERICAN BISON

Body length: 12.4 ft.
Shoulder height: up to 9.5 ft.
Weight: 1800 lbs. (male)
      1200 lbs. (female)
Saved from extinction by conservation

ANDEAN CONDOR

Largest bird of prey
Length beak to tail: 47–51 in.
Wingspan: 10–11.5 ft.

ARABIAN CAMEL

Body length: 7.2–11 ft.
Height at hump: 6.2–7.5 ft.
Weight: 990–1430 lbs.
Extinct as a wild animal

ARABIAN ORYX

Smallest and rarest oryx
Body length: 5.2 ft.
Shoulder height: 32–40 in.
Weight: 140–165 lbs.
Endangered but saved from extinction by conservation

BACTRIAN CAMEL

Body length: 7.5–11.2 ft.
Height at humps: 6.2–7.5 ft.
Weight: 990–1435 lbs.
Vulnerable

BEAVER

Largest rodent in N. Hemisphere
Body length: 29–50 in.
Tail length: 10–20 in.
Weight: 25–65 lbs.

BIGHORN SHEEP

Body length: 4–6 ft.
Height: 37–43 in.
Weight: 125–308 lbs.
Vulnerable

BOTTLE-NOSED DOLPHIN

Length: 11–12.8 ft.
Weight: 330–440 lbs.

BULLFROG

Largest N. American frog
Body length: 3.5–8 in.

CHEETAH

Body length: 3.6–5 ft.
Tail length: up to 30 in.
Speed: up to 70 mph
Endangered (Asiatic subspec.)
Vulnerable (African subspec.)

CHIMPANZEE

Best tool-user after man, and one of his closest relatives
Height: 1.2–5.5 ft.
Weight: 90–110 lbs. (male)
      65 lbs. (female)
Vulnerable

COMMON TEAL

Smallest surface-feeding duck
Length beak to tail: c. 14 in.
Wingspan: c. 24 in.

EMPEROR PENGUIN

Largest penguin
Height: c. 4 ft.
Weight: 94 lbs.

EUROPEAN BADGER

Body length: 25–30 in.
Weight: 22–26 lbs.

FENNEC FOX

Smallest of the foxes and has the biggest ears
Body length: 10–16 in.
Ear length: up to 6 in.
Weight: 1.8–3.3 lbs.

GIANT PANDA

Body length: 4–5 ft.
Tail length: 5 in.
Weight: 220–330 lbs.
Endangered

GIBBON

Body length: 16–23 in.
Weight: 12.5 lbs.

GIRAFFE

Tallest mammal
Shoulder height: up to 11 ft.
Weight: 0.9–2.1 tons (male)
      0.6–1.3 tons (female)
At birth: c. 6.5 ft. (height)
      c. 150 lbs. (weight)

GOLDEN EAGLE

Most numerous large eagle
Length beak to tail: 30–35 in.
Wingspan: 6.5 ft.

GORILLA

Largest and heaviest ape
Height: 5.5–6 ft. (male)
      4.5–5 ft. (female)
Weight: 310–400 lbs. (male)
      200 lbs. (female)
Endangered (Mountain spec.)
Vulnerable (Lowland spec.)

GRAY KANGAROO

Height: up to 4 ft.
At birth: 0.03 oz. (weight)
      c. 0.8 in. (length)
Jump record: 44.3 ft. (length)
      10.5 ft. (height)

GRAY SEAL

Length head to tail: 7 ft. (male)
      6 ft. (female)
Weight: up to 485 lbs. (male)
      c. 330 lbs. (female)

GRAY SQUIRREL

Body length: 9–12 in.
Tail length: 8–9 in.

GREATER ROADRUNNER

Length beak to tail: 20–23.5 in.
Tail length: 12 in.
Speed: up to 15 mph

GREAT INDIAN RHINOCEROS

Body length: 12–12.5 ft.
Height: 5.6–6.1 ft.
Weight: 2.4 tons
Endangered

GREAT WHITE SHARK

Largest flesh-eating shark
Length: 20–33 ft.
Weight: estimated up to 7 tons

GREEN TURTLE

Length: 40–50 in. (female)
Weight: c. 500 lbs. (female)
Endangered

GREEN WOODPECKER

Length beak to tail: c. 12.5 in.
Wingspan: c. 16 in.
Weight: c. 7 oz.

HARVEST MOUSE

Smallest European rodent
Body length: 2–3 in.
Tail length: 2–3 in.
Weight: 0.21 oz. (male)
      0.25 oz. (female)

HAZEL DORMOUSE

Body length: 3–3.4 in.
Tail length: 2–3 in.

HIPPOPOTAMUS

Length: 10.8–11.3 ft.
Height: 4.5 ft.
Weight: 1.8–3.5 tons

IMPALA

Body length: c. 4.5 ft.
Tail length: 12 in.
Shoulder height: 282–300 in.
Jump record: 33 ft. (length)
      10 ft. (height)

INDIAN ELEPHANT

Second largest land mammal (after African elephant)
Body length: 18–21 ft.
Weight: 5.5 tons
Weight at birth: 240 lbs.
Endangered

JACK RABBIT

Not a true rabbit—a hare
Body length: 18–24.5 in.
Ear length: c. 5.5 in.
Speed: up to 35 mph

KOALA

Length: 28–30 in.
Weight: 17.5–26 lbs.

LION

Body length: 8.5–10.8 ft. (male)
Tail length: 25–30 in.
Weight: 330–530 lbs. (male)
270–400 lbs. (female)

MERRIAM'S KANGAROO RAT

Body length: 4.8–6.3 in.
Tail length: 7–8.5 in.
Weight: 3–4.8 oz.

MOOSE

Largest of the deer
Body length: 8.2–10 ft.
Shoulder height: 5.5–7.5 ft.
Weight: 880–1760 lbs.

NILE CROCODILE

Length: 15–16.5 ft.
Weight: 900–1150 lbs.
Vulnerable

OKAPI

Height: 5–5.5 ft.
Weight: 460–550 lbs.

ORANGUTAN

Second largest ape
Height: 4.5 ft. (male)
3.5 ft. (female)
Endangered

OSTRICH

Largest bird
Lays largest egg
Height: up to 9 ft.
Weight: up to 345 lbs.
Egg weight: 3.5–4lbs.

PALLAS'S SANDGROUSE

Length beak to tail: 13.5–15.5 in.
Weight: c. 9.5 oz.
Wingspan: 24.5–30.5 in.

PINE MARTIN

Body length: 13.5–22.5 in.
Tail length: 8.5–11 in.
Weight: 2.2–3 lbs.

PLAINS ZEBRA

Body length: 7.5 ft.
Tail length: 20 in.
Weight: 520 lbs.

POLAR BEAR

Largest carnivorous
quadruped
Body length: 8–10 ft. (male)
5–8 ft. (female)
Weight: 770–1300 lbs. (male)
385–660 lbs (female)
Vulnerable

RABBIT

Body length: 13.5–17.5 in.
Tail length: 1.75–3 in.
Weight: 3–6.5 lbs.
Ear length: 2–2.7 in.

RACCOON

Body length: 19.5–23.5 in.
Tail length: 7.8–15.5 in.
Weight: 11–18 lbs.

RED FOX

Body length: up to 25 in.
Tail length: up to 17.5 in.
Weight: 10–13 lbs.

RED PANDA

Body length: 20–25 in.
Tail length: 11–19 in.
Weight: 6.5–11 lbs.

ROE DEER

Smallest native European deer
Body length: 35–50 in.
Shoulder height: 25–35 in.
Weight: 35–50 lbs.

SCARLET MACAW

Length beak to tail: c. 35 in.

SLENDER LORIS

Body length: 7–10 in.
Weight: 7–10.5 oz.

SPECTACLED BEAR

Only S. American bear
Body length: 5–6 ft.
Weight: 285–440 lbs. (male)
75–140 lbs. (female)
Vulnerable

SPERM WHALE

Largest of toothed whales
Length: c. 70 ft. (male)
c. 40 ft. (female)
Weight: 50–75 tons (male)
16–22 tons (female)

SPOTTED CUSCUS

Body length: c. 28 in.
Tail length: c. 12 in.

STRIPED SKUNK

Body length: 11–15 in.
Tail length: c. 12 in.
Weight: 3–6.5 lbs.

THORNY DEVIL

Length: c. 6.2 in.

TIGER

Largest of the big cats
Weight: 400–570 lbs. (male)
285–350 lbs. (female)
Endangered

VICUNA

Smallest member of camel
family
Length: 4.5–5 ft.
Shoulder height: 33.5–37.5 in.
Weight: 100–120 lbs.
Vulnerable

WALRUS

Body length: 8.5–10.5 ft. (male)
8–9 ft. (female)
Tusk length: 14–20 in. (male)
9–16 in. (female)
Weight: 1750–2660 lbs. (male)
1240–1830 lbs. (female)

Index